rock

rock

rock

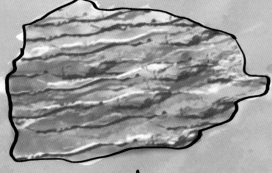

rock

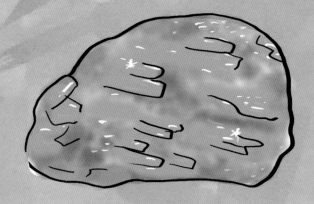

rock

rock

rock

rock

For Mike and Leo Barton (family hug!)

This book would not have been possible without
the knowledge (and patience!) of Billyjack Jory: Geologist,
U.S. Marine, Leadman, & Rock Book Consultant.

VIKING
An imprint of Penguin Random House LLC, New York

First published in the United States of America by Viking, an imprint of Penguin Random House LLC, 2020

Visit us online at penguinrandomhouse.com

LIBRARY OF CONGRESS CATALOGING-IN-PUBLICATION DATA IS AVAILABLE
ISBN 9780451480958

Manufactured in China

3 5 7 9 10 8 6 4 2

The artwork in this book was created using Higgins inks on paper, Photoshop CC (I heart Kyle Brushes),
and Rebelle 3. The main text was lettered with hand-carved bamboo calligraphy pens (that I bought
on the street outside Shanghai) and ink. Soundtrack provided by OmWriter.

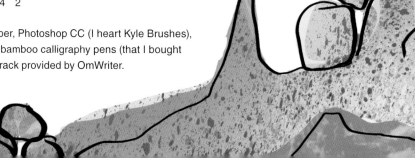

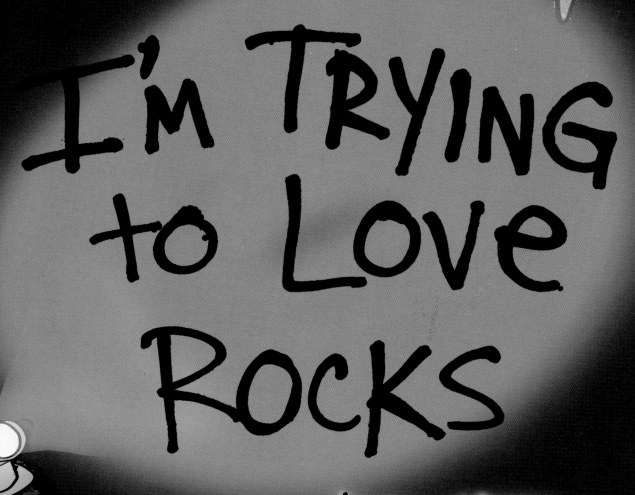

I'm TRYING to Love ROCKS

WORDS & PICTURES by bethany bARTon

VIKING

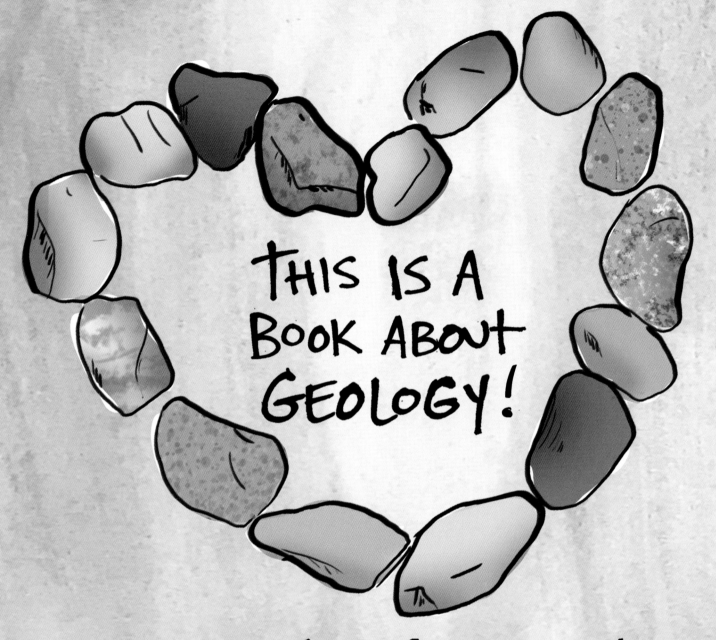

THIS IS A BOOK ABOUT GEOLOGY!

AND IT ALL STARTS WITH LOVING ROCKS! LIKE THAT ROCK RIGHT OVER THERE.

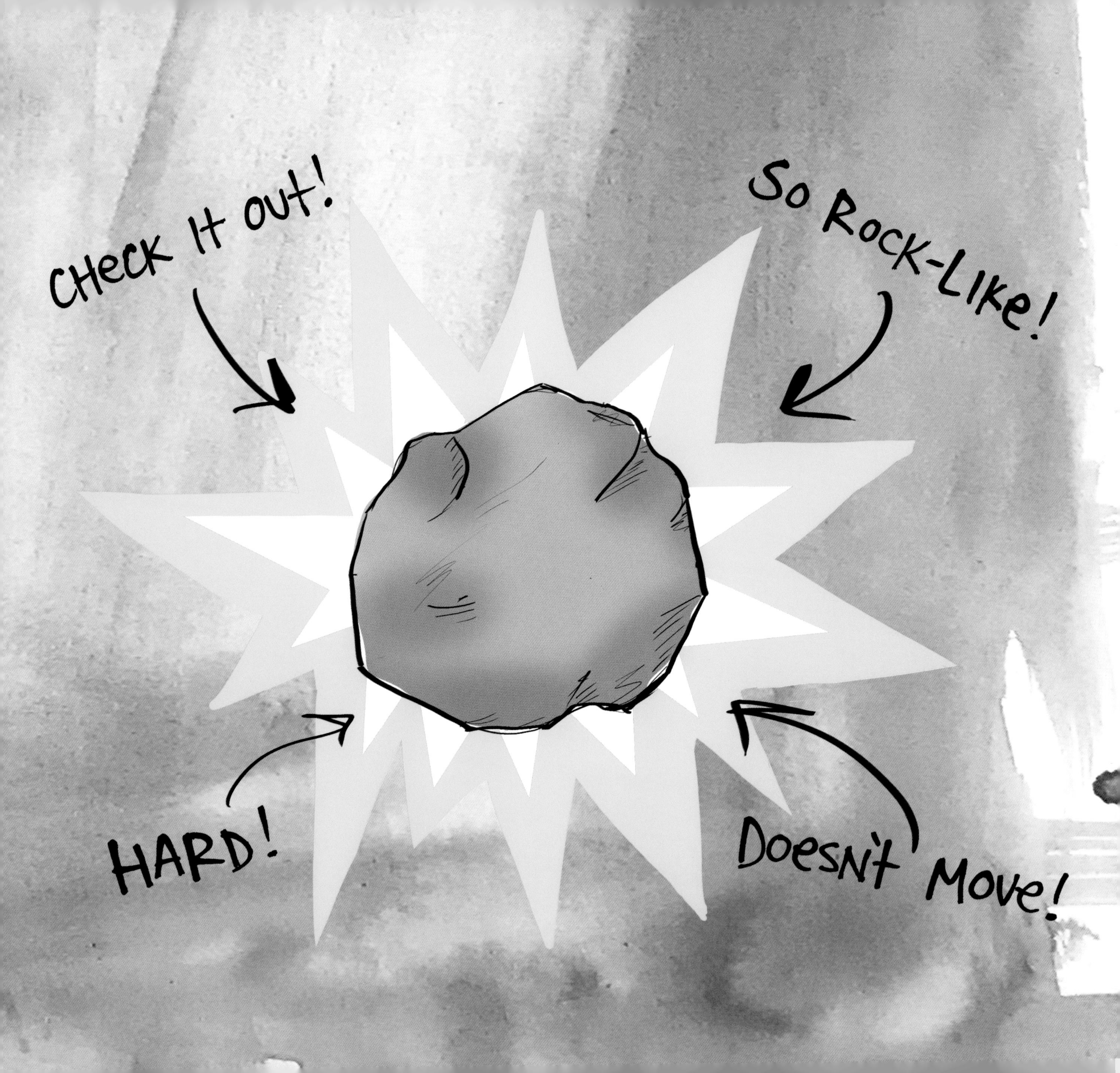
CHECK IT OUT!
SO ROCK-LIKE!
HARD!
DOESN'T MOVE!

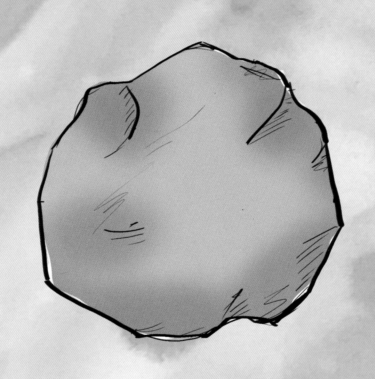

HMMM...It TURNS OUT ROCKS
DON'T REALLY DO MUCH.

MAYBE WE SHOULD POKE IT?

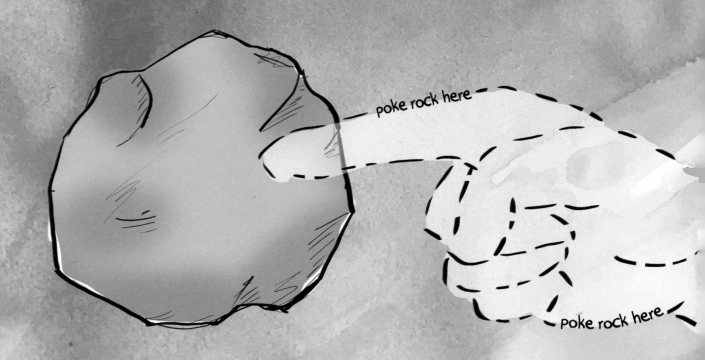

...It's still not doing anything.

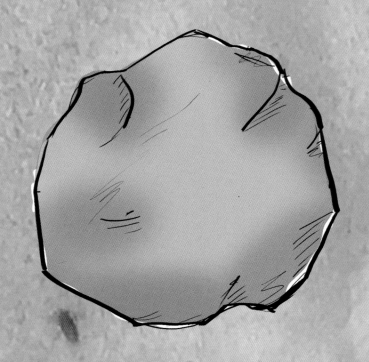

Welp, that didn't work.
Maybe the next book will be better.

THE END.

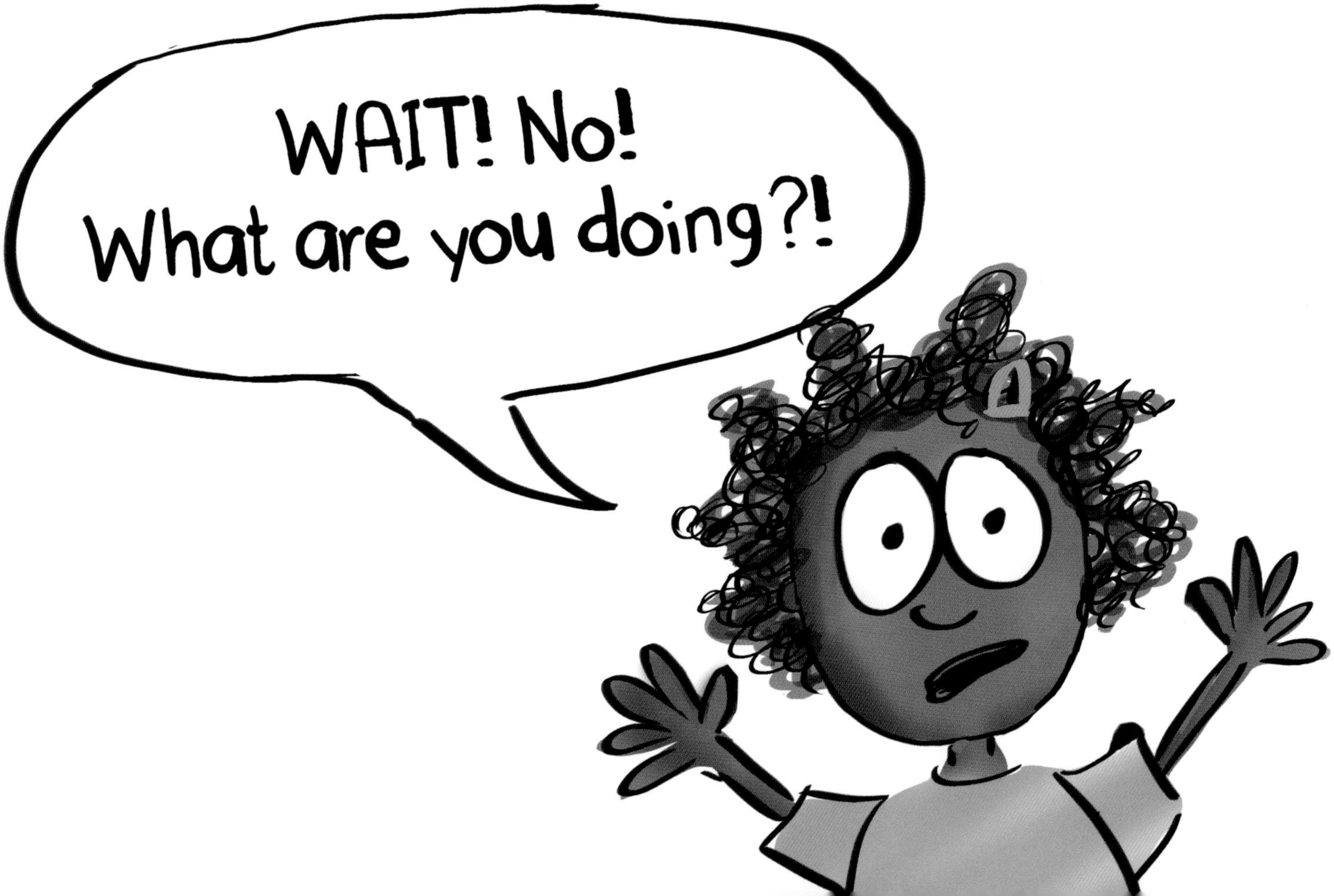

NO WAY.

Really! Geology is more than just staring at rocks.

Geology is the study of what the earth is made of. . .

the relatively thin plates of solid rock we live on!

mostly solid rock called peridotite, with some areas of hot melty rock

liquid super-hot rock, iron, & nickel (4,000-5,000 Celsius)

solid super-hot iron & nickel (around 6,000 Celsius!) that's under too much pressure to melt!

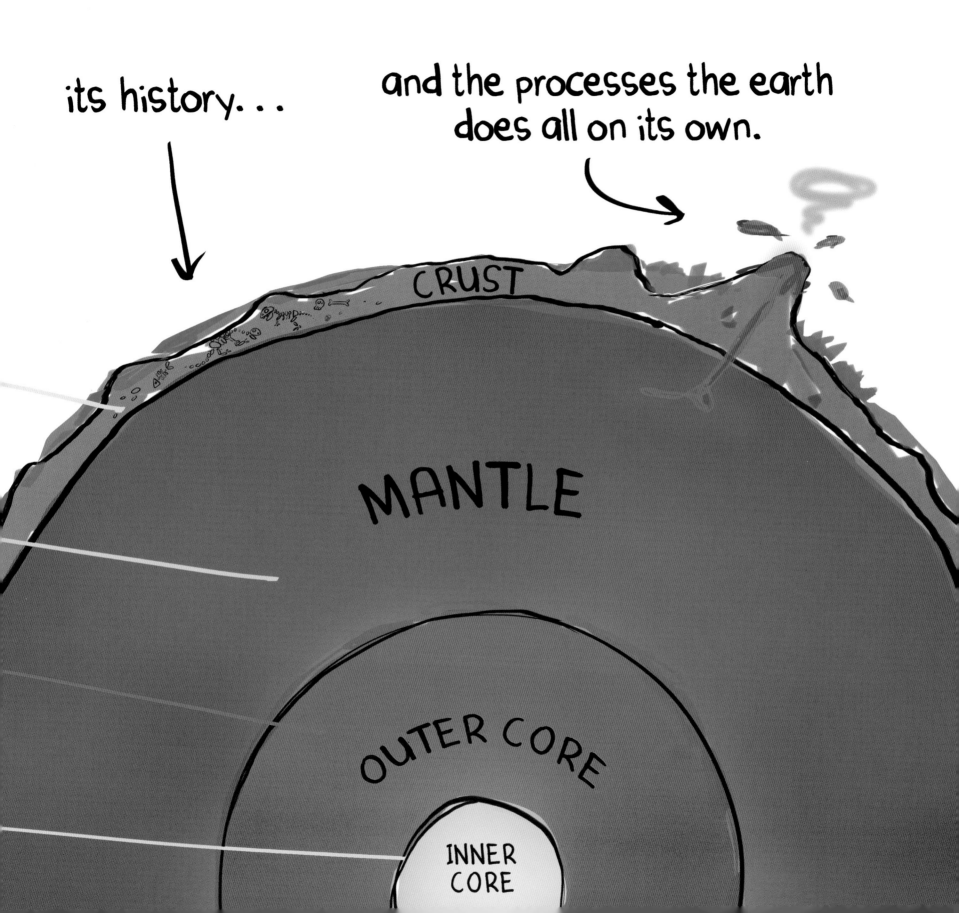

Wow! So you can make me love rocks?

I can try! Check this out:

They might not look like they're doing much, but all rocks on Earth are constantly (and super slowly) changing, with the help of:

weathering,

pressure,

and heat!

OKAY, FIERY LIQUID ROCK IS EASY to LOVE.

BUT WHAT ABOUT ALL tHE BORING ROCKS I See EVERY DAY?

(YAWN.)

But these rocks all have different stories to tell!

WAIT, ROCKS CAN TALK?
WHY DIDN'T YOU tell Me?
HELLO, ROCKS! NICE to Meet you!
WHAT ARE YOUR NAMES?

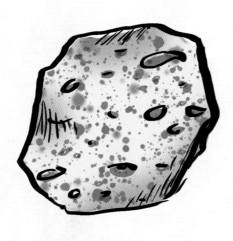

THEY'RE NOt TALKING.

Over many, many years, the earth breaks down and changes each type of rock into new and different rock. We call this:

THE ROCK CYCLE

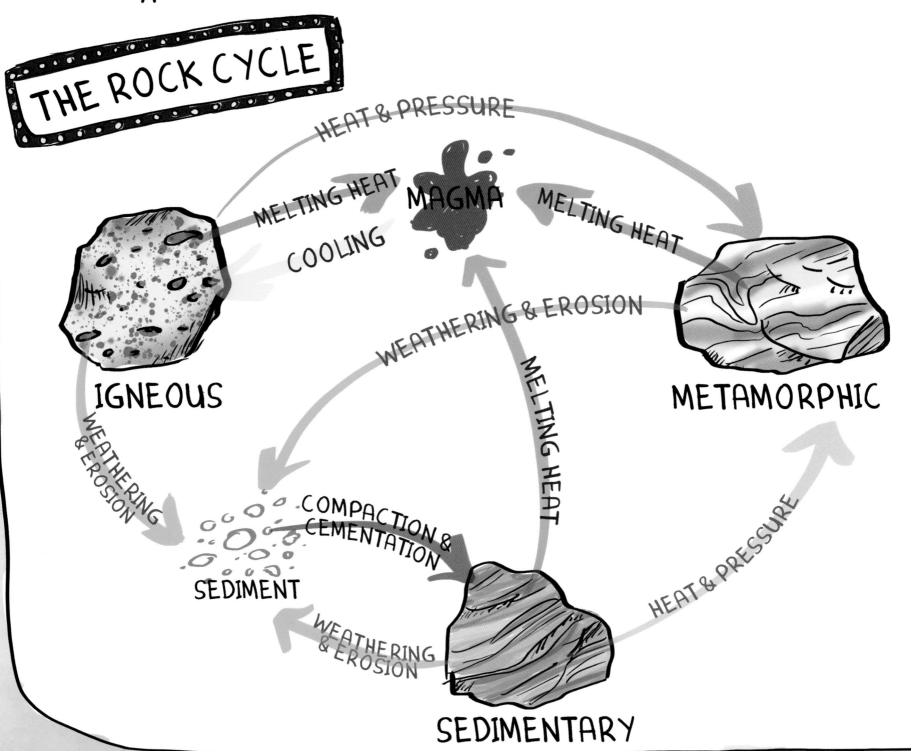

HEAT & PRESSURE

MELTING HEAT

MAGMA

MELTING HEAT

COOLING

IGNEOUS

WEATHERING & EROSION

METAMORPHIC

WEATHERING & EROSION

MELTING HEAT

COMPACTION & CEMENTATION

SEDIMENT

HEAT & PRESSURE

WEATHERING & EROSION

SEDIMENTARY

The word "igneous" means fiery, because igneous rocks are formed when hot melted rock cools . . .

either underground . . .
magma becomes intrusive rock, like this granite

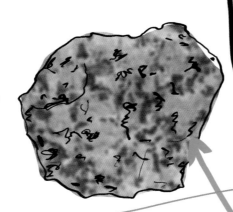

or because of a volcanic eruption!

lava becomes extrusive rock, like this obsidian

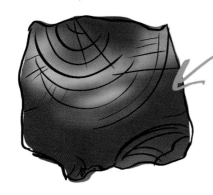

Most of the earth's crust is igneous rock.

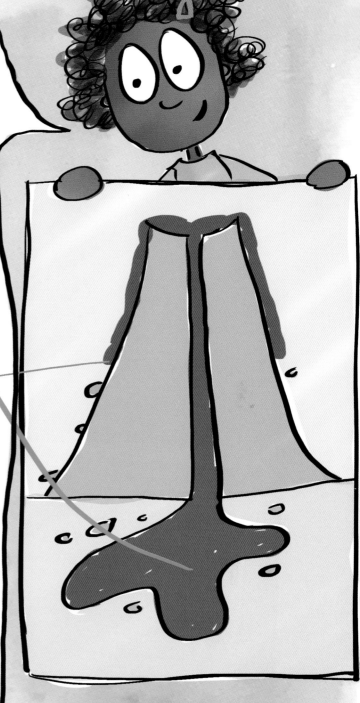

THAT'S A LOTTA LAVA!

Sedimentary rock is made of ... wait for it ... sediment!

Weathering from wind, sand, and water breaks rock up into tiny pieces.

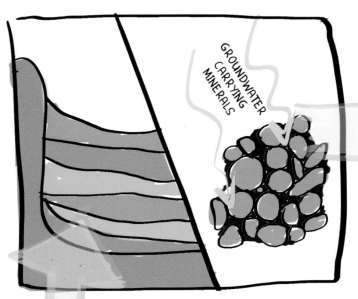

Then comes cementation! That's where dissolved minerals fill in the cracks and glue all the pieces together.

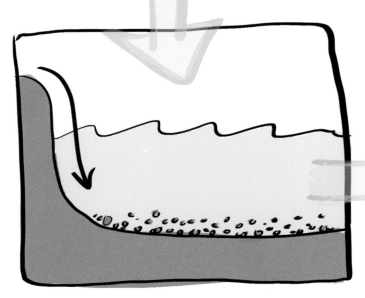

Erosion moves the sediment until it settles into layers.

Layers (or strata) build up over time, and become tightly pressed together. We call that compaction.

Sedimentary rocks sometimes preserve plant and animal remains within their layers.

When minerals replace that organic material . . . we get fossils!

The Grand Canyon is a great example of sedimentary rocks that formed over millions of years.

Metamorphic rock is rock that changes from extreme heat or pressure.

LIMESTONE becomes . . .

MARBLE

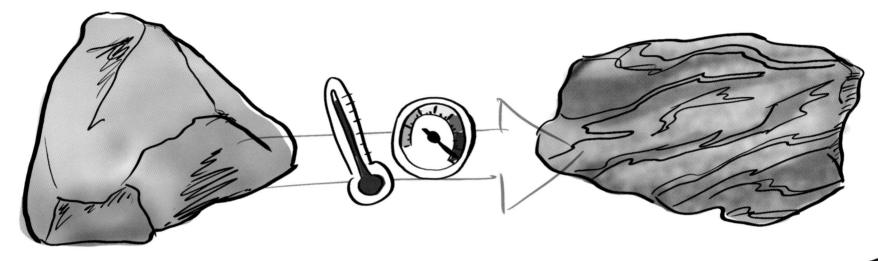

Kind of like how KERNELS become . . .

POPCORN!

And you think that's impressive?

Enter MINERALS and GEMSTONES!

Oooo! SO SPARKLY!

Minerals are the building blocks of rocks and gemstones.

Some minerals we use every day,

like copper,

salt (halite),

or iron.

Other minerals get polished into fancy gemstones.

Many gemstones are created when minerals collect inside and between rocks (usually with the help of water).

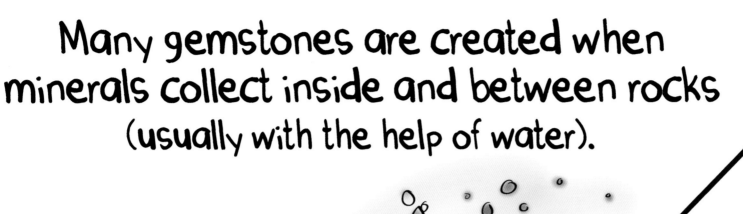

MINERALS

Diamonds are created when carbon is put under extreme pressure.

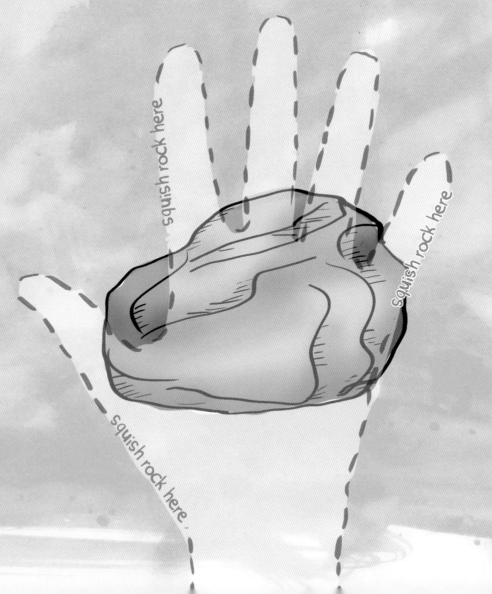

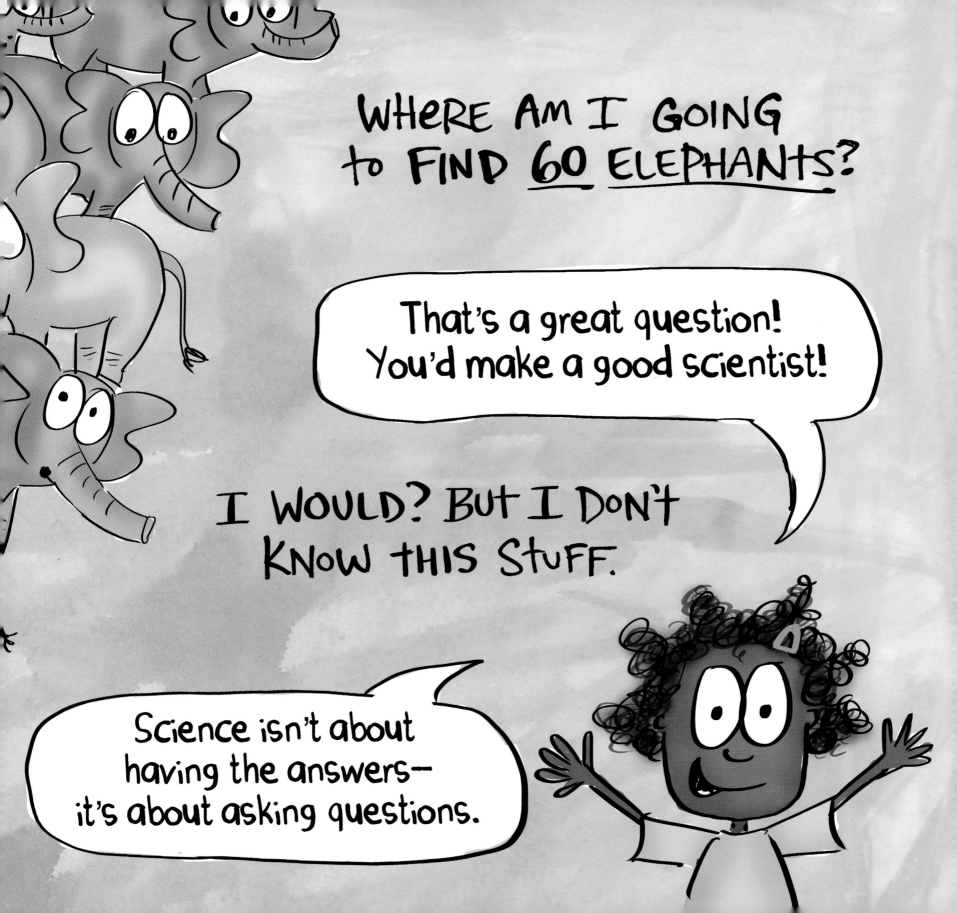

Geologists get to ask lots of big questions about our home, the earth.

How did these mountains get here?

Why do we have earthquakes?

Tectonic plates are huge slabs of rock within the earth's crust. They can shift and sometimes even collide, which is how the Himalayan mountains were formed.

We feel earthquakes when tectonic plates move suddenly along a break or fault.

Think of rocks and minerals as the clues geologists use to figure out the mysteries of our planet.

What will we find if we dig a hole here?

Where did this island come from?

Geologists help find oil and water deep within the layers of Earth's strata.

Many islands are formed when lava from underwater volcanoes cools and builds up enough to create new land!

...and act like time machines,
showing you what the earth looked like
thousands or even millions of years ago.

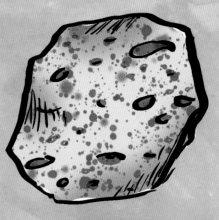
pumice

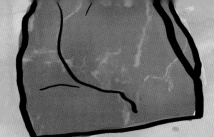
basalt

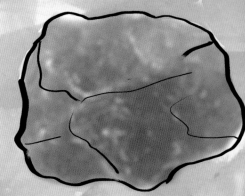
rose quartz

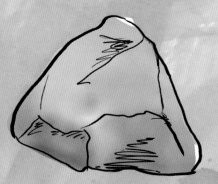
limestone

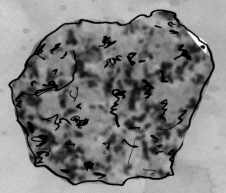
granite

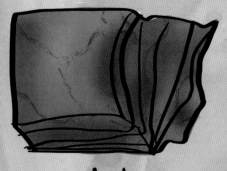
slate

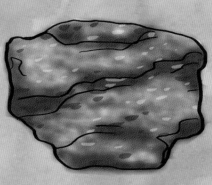
schist

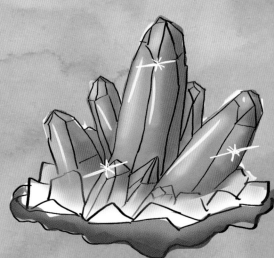
amethyst